FLIRTATION WITH DESTINY

*A SUPERNATURAL JOURNEY
INTO ANOTHER WORLD*

BERNARD THIEMANN

This book is dedicated with love to my family and the heavenly beings who helped shape the moments that live between these pages.

A very special thank you to my dear friend Lela who supported and helped me to launch this book to the world.

FLIRTATION WITH DESTINY

A SUPERNATURAL JOURNEY INTO ANOTHER WORLD

BERNARD THIEMANN

Production Manager: Lela Stojackovic
Publishing Editor: Samantha Fin, The Fin-ish

First published in Australia by Bernard Thiemann with the assistance of
The Fin-ish, 2023.

Copyright © 2023 by Bernard Thiemann

Illustrations by Lela Stojackovic
Edited by Samantha Fin

This book is protected by copyright law.
No reproduction without permission.

The right of Bernard Thiemann to be identified as the author of this
work has been asserted by the relevant worldwide copyright laws.

Bernard Thiemann: bernardthiemann@outlook.com

ISBN (paperback): 978-0-6486974-5-9
ISBN (e-book): 978-0-6486974-3-5

Printed and bound in Australia by Ingram Spark

Flirtation with Destiny reveals aspects to the hidden side of life, one that re-establishes a divine connection with our true, higher-self. The ability to view creation with a broader perspective inspires a rise in consciousness that in turn, enables us to adjust to the realms of infinity.

As we begin to explore and define reality, our human intelligence begins to understand existence and values. My objective herein, is to share my personal and abnormal experiences that have led me on an adventure in search for the truth; recovering forgotten memories that have been mysteriously erased from our past, and from our human consciousness.

Throughout these pages, I have aimed to expose insights that will connect the Self and forge deeper associations with existing, eternal realities. It is a soul-wise journey that presents unique and uplifting surprises, promoting a realization that can make the world of the living more understandable.

May the readers of this book welcome goodness into your lives, more soul-light to the mind, and enjoy a more meaningful and peaceful existence.

Bernard Thiemann

CONTENTS

CHAPTER ONE — 9
INSIDE MY REALITY

CHAPTER TWO — 17
A GLIMPSE OF ETERNITY

CHAPTER THREE — 29
THE GREAT AWAKENING

CHAPTER FOUR — 41
FINE DINING WITH FRIENDS

CHAPTER FIVE — 50
A MIDNIGHT DREAM

CHAPTER SIX — 61
DEATH HAS NO DEATH

CHAPTER SEVEN — 72
SEDUCED BY A MUNDANE ILLUSION

CHAPTER EIGHT — 83
CAUGHT THE WRONG TRAIN TO NOWHERE

CHAPTER NINE — 92
HUMANITY AND HEAVEN

CHAPTER TEN — 101
THE FINAL DISCLOSURE

ABOUT THE AUTHOR — 112

CHAPTER ONE
INSIDE MY REALITY

Within the fields of my mind, drifted a restless wind that was seeking to unravel the secrets of life. To recapture forgotten memories that seemed to have been somehow erased from human consciousness. The vital intelligence connected with the unseen, invisible realities that holds a considerable influence in how we could see ourselves in a higher sense of awareness, ultimately, gaining a greater sense to who we are and why we are.

Throughout the following pages, I have described many of my own personal experiences, including certain passages involving supernatural encounters and astral visitations, highlighting a connection with an invisible world. A deep knowing, allows the Self a unique realization; one that tells us that we are simultaneously interconnected with two existences- our physical creation and the spiritual reality.

We are immortal beings traversing the cosmos, encountering the earthly plane in an experience to enhance soul growth. The development of soul, becoming self-empowered with psychic mediumistic, intuitive qualities to experience soul consciousness is a reality that is divinely inspired. We are the participants on an inspirational journey to reveal our true nature, to assert and identify where we stand with the universe.

I saw it appropriate to have this inclination, a strong yearning, a noble desire to form my own view on 'reality' with substantial evidence gained through personal experience that went well beyond the *physicality* confinement. I believe it is the intention to initiate soul advancement, to stand on common ground with God, with Source. This is, quite literally, achieving spiritual satisfaction. A oneness and alignment with our soul, the essential substance that gave the human image intelligence- the character capability to love and to be creative.

**

In the naturalistic world governed by institutional formalities, the human persona is subjected to a variety of belief systems, where human innocence is induced into a reality to comply with customary habits. This is the way we all learn to embrace an already established empire where one becomes a prisoner to circumstances, until we have reached a higher level of consciousness, that has the foresight to question the integrity of reality that the human mind has created.

When there is so much insecurity and foolishness, control endures, and that combined, has created a dysfunctional, unstable world. Essentially, we are who we are, confined to this reality, however, this doesn't mean that we are denied a choice to change- to question why it is so. This all comes back to the individual, to solve, to give back the world a soul, and a righteousness to think deeper beyond the limits of an ordinary mind.

Over the course of my journey, I came to question that without any spiritual substance, what else is there to expect other than incurring an unsatisfactory inhumane outcome? What needs to be acknowledged, is that living isn't just all about the functions of an outside world, but how we manage the ascendancy into consciousness to attain the truth about us and life itself.
In maintaining a physical spiritual balance with God and with our soul, we advance further into spiritual awareness to understand and master the state of being, promoting the expansion of consciousness. We live in a progressive timeline, evolving within the experiences to form our own conclusions, being mindful to stay true to our oneness. All the while experiencing the ways of the spirit, the scope, and the creation of the wonder of love.

The path to self-enlightenment is where human consciousness emerges with divine consciousness to embrace our inner world to gain a clearer understanding of who we are.

**

To form a personal relationship with the universe, to arise from a common lifestyle, to discover who you are, exists a good deal of randomness. For it is you who shapes your destiny, it is you who creates the way you think and feel, and you who decides whether to climb the heights of life or remain in spiritual stagnation- ultimately leading towards nowhere.

Nonetheless, people have an obligation to protect the living environment, to keep the mind healthy, the soul protected from all negativities, and to uphold an honest living; protecting the integrity and values that are designed to preserve the human civilization.

In the midst of all things occurring in life, what needs to be understood is that the universe wants us to be safe and prosperous, but to also teach us lessons in order for us to evolve and mature to a level that exceeds the normal range of awareness. In the common view, the mainstream population is generally involved with creative activities, a working life, social living that tends to give the impression of realistic realism.

Naturalistically, sooner or later people are bound to question the existence that would render the focus more on theological feelings- for the higher-self to emerge. This is, on an individual level, where we take ownership in the sense to become soul wise.

Understanding that we are to emerge as divine beings by perfecting the human nature, dealing with our own karma, to heal the Self and to evolve in the way that holds merit and intellectual forwardness to reach our natural destiny.

The reality is that every human being is a carrier of his own universe within; a sacred place that is timeless where the Self can establish a unified relationship with the celestial heavens. This is where the transformation begins and is the rise of the human being becoming spiritual. It is a true love story that characterizes a personal involvement with the continuity of creationism.

**

This book is a window into my world, a world that that has shaped my reality based on life *living* and *being*. A journey that encouraged the intellect to break free from the grips of a conditioned mind to sense my own original personality. The rekindling of supernatural powers to gain further spiritual knowing, retrieving the hidden secrets of life.

To be you, means experiencing soul advancement including the awareness of the afterlife. Knowing is better than ignorance and to leave everything in control of fate wasn't an option for me. I wanted to be in control of my destiny, developing my spiritual nature in the faith of prayers, meditation, dreams, mediumistic stimulations, and spirit guidance to stay in touch with God and the wonders of His love. The human story is eternal; we are the pilgrims, the explorers, and how each person handles the journey will depend on their choices and decisions, ultimately determining their destiny.

CHAPTER TWO
A GLIMPSE OF ETERNITY

"The human spirit descended upon the wings of light from beyond the higher heavens with a divine image firmly entrenched within his soul, the individual venturing into a classroom filled with disguise indifferences and deceptions while the mind was in search for its soul inside the human realm of redemption."

The campfire was alight, and a small triangular shape tent was erected for an overnight stay within a secluded, countryside valley. It felt good to be on country to camp and relax within the natural environment. Here the valley stood in silence except for the sound of burning twigs and firewood. It was time to be alone to interact with my thoughts; heartfelt feelings that wanted to connect with my soul.

The day was about to end, and behind, a blue sky awaited the night that stood in readiness to transform daylight into darkness. As expected within the hour, daylight began to gradually fade, while in the distance, a noticeably red and orange tinted skyline, scented with feathery clouds that lazily floated in front of a radiant sun, gracefully descended beyond the endless horizon.

Serenity filled the meadows, and the darkness covered the entire landscape as the valley fell asleep. Moments later, above the campsite, an outstretched heaven displayed a visible magical spectrum of infinity; a timeless deep-space manifestation that exposed distant clusters of sparkling lights, giving the night sky a sense of life. Upon witnessing, one could argue that the whole nature of creation was just a wild fantasy dream; a creative masterpiece granting existence, character, imagination, and intelligence.

**

There must be a genuine purpose for the human being to bring a personal touch into life, to co-exist with a superimposed reality. A genuine reason to have an infinite relationship and a genuine involvement with a gigantic masterpiece. This timeless divine sanctum of infinite space, that was dominated by endless luminous star constellations, defined a massive creational structure that initially could only have been devised by a Superimposed Intelligence Source.

It was too awesome even to comprehend this eternalness that gave the human image a soul, a heartbeat, the essential life force, to have a life in conscious awareness.

The night had now reached full blackness and more firewood was needed to keep the flames alive to surround the cold darkness with warmth and light. Here I was in contemplation with my inner thoughts still trying to comprehend the soul's immortality, the fulfilment the purpose, and the destiny.

I thought about how we know a lot about the physical world, but little is understood about ourselves, our feelings and the mind's potentiality. Instead, in general, the human focus is glued to an established outside world, in the hope to have a successful life.

The uncertainty arises at the end of the physical life, but what then? Do we know what will happen then? The end sparks the beginning of a reunification with a world that is enshrined in secrecy.

The mind held another thought as I pondered upon the reincarnation factor or system in the transition from one existence to another. What puzzled me was how it can be possible to find oneself here, on a liveable planet that floated unhinged and unaided in the cosmos of space.

**

What was also mystifying to me was our planet's daily rotation, the yearly orbit around the celestial sun, the whole systematic momentum that remained unfelt and un-noticed, leaving the human mindfully unaware of such continuous movement.

The question that stood in my mind, was why I had found myself here on this particular planet when the galaxies and solar systems held countless of planetary systems. Maybe, it was chosen for a reason to fulfil certain karmic obligations developing further into consciousness, or perhaps, to be given the opportunity to learn more about peace and love.

Embracing the soul's strength and its unimaginable powers is the unlimited reach the mind has in order to remain fully connected with all that is existing. Deny this strength and the human mind will stay stuck inside a third-dimensional hologram that has institutionalized individuality into a humanized program, tricking the mind into a false-narrative perception, predominately controlled by power and greed.

Nevertheless, we don't need to remain completely locked down and conform to an earthbound, mundane reality when we have the spiritual empowerment and the gifts to ascend the human awareness into higher fields of consciousness.

That night, gazing into deep space, the above universe exposed a visible glimpse of eternity, an endless eternalness. Here my mind was wondering where to find this afterlife, the spirit world, the heavenly kingdom, as this will one day become our futuristic destiny. Then I thought about the moment of death. What will happen to me? How will I end up somewhere in another existence that had remained invisible to the rational mind?

**

Why has the spirit world become so invisible, when the mind has unlimited reach, soul-wise intelligence, and spiritual powers to make direct connections with the afterlife? Is it that we are disinterested, afraid, and superstitious of the unknown that exists outside the normal range of physical reality? Finding God and understanding a broader picture of reality, is what would give human intelligence a realistic and authentic way of being.

What I had clearly felt that night, camped beneath the blanket of twinkling stars, was the countryside, the energy, the peace, and the stillness of the night. It had captured my imagination and inspired a feeling of oneness with life. The night sky will always remain the same, reappearing when daylight moves to another part of the world and providing the moments to live to sleep to dream.

Then, with a new sunrise, the physical journey continues to wrestle with problems, relationships, and learning the art of love and compassion. Then the night reappears to dream of the spirit life.
Day and night- the physical and the spiritual connections are felt.

We find that within us there exists a spiritual power; the divine intelligence that has no boundaries or limitations in which it continues to hold in one hand, a physical world and in the other, the spirit world. It is a connection of love.

It was time for the night universe to fade and disappear from the sky as the morning had broken, bursting into life with natural sunlight, as I packed my belongings to drive back home to normality.

Now this was an interesting, unusual moment in my life, in the times of spiritual development. Speaking of planetary star systems and the cosmic universe, this is what happened: I had joined a meditation spiritual group where the meetings were held one day weekly. On this occasion in the meditation, I experienced being on board a spacecraft.

**

I should point out that both the group, and myself knew, about celestial beings and the existence of spaceships; the watchers, those who oversaw the development of humanity. The meditation commenced in the usual manner, the attention focused on the third eye, internal viewing screen, when immediately the viewing become alive, and I saw myself walking around inside a metallic circular designed spacecraft. I heard a voice asking me where I wanted to go and without a thought, I replied: "To the moon". I didn't see his presence, but I felt the sincerity in his male voice, so I concluded that he must be the commander of the spacecraft.

The moon came into my thoughts due to the short time available before the meditation session ended. I thought the craft would handle the distance in quick time. During my time on board, I entered a large room and at precisely that moment, a female crew member, wearing a grey bluish uniform came up to me carrying a tray with a welcoming drink resting on top. It looked a lot like a champagne glass filled with an orangey-colored mixture and when I tasted it, it felt smooth and easy to drink.

Then, I heard the same voice again, instructing me to look outside through a rounded shape window. To my astonishment, I saw the moon's surface at close range. I estimated the craft was hovering approximately fifty to seventy miles above the surface.

The voice mentioned that not many humans from earth had seen the backside of the moon. I stood in wonder of the size of the huge craters with so many of them indented into the moon surface. And just like that I was back in physical consciousness, looking back up at the sky; transfixed and contemplating my flight episode to the moon.

My experience was just a fleeting moment on board a particular spacecraft. I wasn't clear why I was chosen, but I felt appreciative to have been able to broaden my understanding of the fact that we are not alone in the universe; that more intelligent, higher technologically advanced, spiritually evolved beings exist, compared with our current state.

**

There was a dream I had in this episode; I saw myself on the surface of another world, just enough to see a short distance above in the sky, where a large, black, triangular spacecraft slowly and gracefully landed at a nearby base. The spectacular view was just magical and so definitively real, and I was in awe of the engineered, transportation flying machine which I imagined could transit throughout the entire universe.

One time, there was an encounter in real-time: a visitation from a different world. I was taking an afternoon nap when suddenly, I awoke and leaned forward to see two extra-terrestrial beings of the grey-species kind. They stood at the end of the bed watching me with their large black piercing eyes. Startled, but unafraid of them I asked instinctively: "What do you want?". Immediately after I spoke, they vanished from my presence.

There was another big and unexpected event, and again this happened in real-time when I was relaxed alone sitting on the bed. Out of the blue, and for no reason I asked myself: "What is going to happen to this world, to our future? Immediately, in clear view, at the end of my bed it happened. Somehow, by divine influence, I began to see a color a projection of the future in that part of the room.

The world was battered by enormous storms and heavy rains, like the world had never experienced before. I saw people rushing to the mountains to find shelter in caves. I saw a sky filled with spacecrafts to evacuate the people stranded. Then, I witnessed the planet being sucked into an enormous cosmic wormhole and watched as it was continuously struck with electrifying, lightning currents- each strike revitalizing the earth with renewed energy.

Then, once on board the rescue craft I was shown people's private accommodation quarters furnished with bed, shower, and toilet.

**

Then I was taken to the dining area, which was a large room, decorated to the equivalent of a five-star dining room hotel. All the tabletops were covered with quality tablecloths and the plates and cutlery equally placed- as if expecting royalty. Then I was shown the auditorium; an enormous lecture facility that could seat hundreds as well as accommodate influential teachers on its stage.

On board, it was a daily routine to attend the educational meetings.

Living on the craft seemed to last a long time, as long it took for a renewed and energized planet to be ready for resettlement. From the craft's windows I saw the once old planet exiting at the other end of the wormhole, sliding into a higher-frequency, galactic universe replaced by beautiful blue planet revitalized with flora, nature, and large oceans and rivers. It was destined for those on the many spaceships to inherit a new earth.

This is where the prophesy ended. A message for a future event that might happen. *Be spiritual, remain strong, have faith, and stay close to God.*

CHAPTER THREE
THE GREAT AWAKENING

"Education is a mighty thing; awareness is an even greater thing, but love is the undisputed highest power in life that dissolves distances, heals people's minds and the magic creates humane feelings that produce goodness and opens the heart to be in oneness with eternity."

A sunrise had arisen from a nightly darkened sky, giving we the people, the recovery time to arise from a self-induced, artificial entrancement- an unawareness of life's higher purpose. As for myself, it was time to have the usual breakfast of black tea with jam and toast as the morning television flickered between breaking news, interviews, and commercials, and while the radio waves hosted continuous musical songs to induce an emotional feeling of belonging to a humanized and created world.

The methods, attachments, and languages give us a reality and timeframe that is strictly controlled by mechanical time rituals and obligations. A continuation to be tightly handcuffed to work finances and family life.

The working network consists of 'rush' hours; cities and roads jammed with traffic and street footpaths grouped with people mostly holding their mobile phones talking to invisible faces. The human mind consumed with what is considered to be normality- a routine turning into a habit, and the firmer we cement the mind into confusion, the more we make living unbearable as a result. Ours is a world turning into an automatic, traumatized, and computerized civilization. The governing institutions are breeding this insensitivity and unfairness as our natural way of life, where *being human* is largely being demoralized by power, control and greed.

**

Since we are living in the age of technology; advancements designed to enhance our intelligence level and connect us more closely with one another, the Self needs to be aware that technology's influence does not disengage the intellect from developing a spiritual mind in order to discover our trueness. There exists the need to tread carefully, to keep an even balance with the physical life and the eternalness of the cosmos.

Daunting as life may seem, the control, the misinformation, and the cruelty that persists in tearing people's hearts and souls apart, subjecting the human soul to be beached beneath the spell of fear and uncertainty, is an instability that shows no sign of spiritual substance nor any collective oneness or solidarity. We are the only ones that can resurrect a fallen reality and regain a proper correction with life, to govern and be responsible for our thoughts and actions. We are the only ones that can find the purpose in giving ourselves a real sense of awareness and a meaningful existence.

It is a highly motivated, technical environment that is controlling our future and our destiny, where we are shown only small amounts of how we can manage our own existence. To feel the essentialness of freedom and duty of self-recognition we need to be wiser of who we are and to live on equal, peaceful terms, where people can evolve humanely, spiritually, and intellectually without causing unequal living standards.

We must remember that we are spiritual beings having a human experience. We have a planet that is ruled by money, greed, and expectations, yet, what some people don't realize, is what the Self reflects outwardly is the condition of one's inner world. In some cases, human intelligence forgetting to evolve with a good heart and mind is practical. In a sense it, is where peoples' wellbeing comes first, instead of inhumane practices, and the profiteering generated by selfishness.

**

So how can we attempt to mend a fractured, unstable world in a practical sense, whilst being supportive, considerate, maintain common sense, think positively humanely, and do no harm to anyone? In a spiritual sense, it is to find your inner peace, develop the powers of the mind, and create your own heaven within a spiritual reality that lives in harmony with the universe. It just isn't helpful for a materialistic empire to function without a conscience and to allow injustice dramas to destroy the very fabric of the human dynasty.

To sustain the quality of life, there should exist the realization to progress with a kind of sentimentality; to nurture the vital essence, the backbone of society- the energy of unconditional love.

To incorporate a higher standard of living to what we always dreamed about, we should have the perception to operate simultaneously with a practical sense supported by a spiritual sense. A river of love that flows through every heart which becomes our greatest protector and the unifier to all things that are a reality.

Traditionally, the person sees mainly a physical reflection of himself, introduced by a practical mind, to operate the physical body. Whereas, hidden from normality, is a spiritual mind holding in their possession a light, astral body. It gives the Self a totality; a dimensional personality that isn't confronted by boundaries or is limited in consciousness, but primarily functions on a higher level of awareness, attached to a cosmic existence- that is infinite and eternal.

To this understanding, there exists no real reason to envision any form of separation (especially between life and death), to be impregnated with the thought of being separated from an invisible heaven or from a secretive God only to await to enter the Kingdom and be judged. In truth we possess the magical powers of soul travel to have brief moments to assess the wider divide of actualities, to be familiarized with the invisible reality.

Wherever we exist, the divine nature is carried within every person, the soul source that remains eternally connected to landscapes of the spirit world.

**

Here I would like to share a brief insight into my life and how I became involved in opening the doorway to the unseen reality of the spiritual way of life. I was born to honest, hardworking, and caring parents and until I was seven, we lived in Germany. I suffered from ill health as a child and on the advice of the doctors, we decided to travel to a much better healing climate, and so we immigrated to Australia. This became our country and our way of life.

In my youth I attended the Christian Brother's College where I learned about religion which resonated with my inner nature. When I turned fourteen, we returned to Germany, where I began an apprenticeship, and after its completion four years later, I returned to Australia, this time alone. My parents followed the following year.

In my early adult years, I married and fathered two children, however, after a while, the marriage failed. This was the first time where I experienced real pain, especially when two young children were involved. I was separated from them. As much I wanted to repair the marriage, it wasn't to be.

Through this ending marked the beginning of new chapter in my life. Fate had taken me on a different road to experience new opportunities. At this moment I became more acquainted with the sensitive, emotional side that exposed a true reflection of my mind. In 1980, I moved from a country town to a coastline city and there my new life began. I made friends with highly regarded mediums and psychics where I learned a higher form of spirituality that gave me a broader view on reality. This became a very important period in my life where I took an interest in philosophical books that were in line with spiritual healing, channeling, astral travelling, the third eye, spirit guides, the chakras and so on.

**

The findings demonstrated the potentiality of the human being literally defining our reality, attracting spiritual energies, neutralizing negative influences, and developing a positive mind in order to find our inner peace and spiritual fulfilment.

From this moment on, I befriended psychics, mediums, and special orientated, spiritually aware individuals who all demonstrated extraordinary spiritual gifts. This, above all, gave me an interest and direction in developing my own, yet dormant, psychic spiritual nature.

In due time, a great awakening occurred to the point where I developed internal vision. This gave me a direct, visible connection with the supernatural worlds. My spiritual eye, or what is better known as the third eye, posted colorful patterns, symbolic images, soul experiences, astral landscapes and even futuristic events as images that would appear in mind's internal viewing screen, situated in the middle of the forehead just above my two normal eyes.

Naturally, I knew that behind the inflowing psychic scenes, stood a higher power, a spirit guidance that was creating a communication link designed to heal the distance between a temporary physical world and the spirit realms. This was my way of developing a positive mind to strengthen a divine accord, with soul intelligence, to the curiosity- fostering a flirtation with destiny.

I have come to believe that we all must become closer to and function with our intuition, to speak our truths, so as to navigate the Self through the valleys of the mind and evolve toward higher states of consciousness. To become a powerful magnet in possession of the key to unlock the secrets of the universe, we must resonate deeper.

Whether, on what level, the human signature emerges from a physical experiment or from supernatural experiences, there always exists the opportunity to find the things that take you to see a brighter version of oneself; an ability to change faith into the truth, darkness into light, and indifferences into love.

**

In time I settled into another relationship that produced another child, however, regrettably this also was short lived and once again I was led to travel on a lonely road. Still, I continued to proceed with the interest in developing my spiritual nature and discovering a firmer foundation to my existence.

In later years, I became involved in a remarkable relationship with a spirited, kind-hearted woman, sharing similar spiritual interests and understanding each other's personality. These interests included the way we wanted to experience the living and how to make our days more enjoyable and lasting. This was to me the basis of a healthy partnership and friendship founded on loyalty and trust.

Foremost, what I had learned from past experiences, is to remember that human feelings evolve as the intellect evolves and the mind (subconsciously or consciously) is always in search of how to perfect existence. The human world that surrounds us isn't a true reflection of who we are, and we are here to find the person of gracious character that resides in us; a personality who is in a natural way intellectually connected with the spiritual orbit yet able to recognize the truth in an eternal belonging.

We are in the position to change an unstable world that hungers for stability, equality, and security- a world that needs peace and happiness. We all can change a negative, unhealthy situation for the better, only when we ourselves transform. It serves no one to live in a sugar-coated civilization in the belief that institutional systems are generally concerned to support the wellbeing of humanity.

What is most important, is not to forsake our identity or our trust in life, but the opportunity to become the person the Self *ought to become*.

CHAPTER FOUR
FINE DINING WITH FRIENDS

*"Served to the dinner table, as requested,
was winter soup, white wine, and fresh salmon,
while a divine persona of the human nature
was seated at another table."*

I always took an interest in trying to make sense of reality, forging a personal quest for self-illumination with fresh ideas that would improve the way the mind thinks. To walk with self-independence, trust impeccable humaneness, and replant the authenticity seeds back into human consciousness.

For me it wasn't enough just to live out a routine lifestyle in the terminology classed as 'certified normality'. I needed to find myself in a healthier frame of mind, in a world where the Self can easily become traumatized with materialistic conquest, to become spiritually lost in modern-day living.

Self-awareness is a unified healing process. To correct and identify the fallacies that have manifested and caused human entrapment throughout time we have to go beyond the invented and imitating characters that live separated from one's higher-self. It is these personas that only exist wanting to measure one's own intellectual power in the realms of a make-believe world; stiving to be an influential personality in the human kingdom.

The evidence is there where it is obvious, the damage that the 'ego' has managed to accomplish, inventing greed, creating poverty, wars, and human injustice. As if someone out there wants us always to live in fear, struggle, hardship and in separation from each other, when the living should be fairer to justify a natural humane living as possible.

**

The more conscious we become of ourselves and the world around us, the more we can feel and comprehend a deeper state of being- an awakening to the rise of the higher-self. We can emerge, rescued from self-induced imprisonment. In general, we exist in a love story gone wrong, where the human heart was betrayed, forcing human nature to fall into spiritual unconsciousness.

An interesting imaginary tale came to mind to illustrate a reality associated with the human character. In the episode, was a young man who decided to have dinner at a designated restaurant, and unbeknownst to him, was accompanied by two personalities, strongly attached to his mind. The man and his two companions, his 'ego intellect' and the 'religious persona' were all seated at the same table.

The waiter came to take the order of requested meals. The young man ordered his choice from the menu: "I'll have the chef's choice of the day- winter soup and fresh salmon served with white wine." The meal cooked was to his satisfaction. Meanwhile his two friends ordered their preferred meals.

The 'ego persona' ordered his chosen meal. What was served: a hot dish of crab short-neck combination soup, an entrée of rocket salad fried wontons with a quantity of nuts, a delicious plate loaded with sauerkraut, and fried devilish sausages with ketchup. The dessert was served: gooseberry grumble scented with a slight touch of superior attitude. The meal was paired with a large gimlet cocktail on the rocks, filled with cracked ice. Overall, the meal went down with a slight hint of indigestion.

**

Meanwhile the 'religious persona' ordered. The meal that was served: a warm dish of soul fish soup, enlightened with a slight sprinkle of garlic. The entrée was a medium serving of Caesar salad with two slices of angel bread, followed by a simple serving of butterfly prawns, and a plate of spicy seasoned chicken with creamy sage sauce and out-of-this-world steamed vegetables. The dessert: a heavenly caramelized citrus Cointreau torte decorated with a religious hint of soul advancement. The meal was paired with a holy drink of rum cocktail 'love potion number nine'. Overall, the meal was a great success that allowed the soul to float above the clouds.

When the feasting was almost done, the Self suddenly recognized, that seated at another table was a very close friend that he once had known quite well. All alone in a secluded corner of the restaurant was a distinguished presence that glowed with a spiritual aura reflecting a high level of integrity. But the young man also noticed an imprint of sadness; a painful sense of betrayal to have been banished from the king's table- the control seat of consciousness. A position that was conquered by a programmed intellectual influence.

The rise of the lower-self, (a pretentious intruder that craved for power), seemed to conspire to manipulate and control in a sinister way to disempower the Self from his greatness.

But now, inside the restaurant, a forgotten memory was rediscovered, and a deep-felt friendship was reunited. The divine image of the higher-self; a most trusted companion and our truest friend was reinstated to claim back his rightful office at the helm of the human personality. Without any further hesitation, the higher-self was invited back to the main table where goodwill and harmony was restored.

**

A spiritual aura now surrounded the human embodiment; a divine intelligence that gave the Self extended powers for the mind to have internal sight, a heart filled with compassion and selflessness, ultimately being given the passport to enter the hidden territories of life.

In celebration, the higher-self ordered his preferred meal from the menu; a generous serve of grace from the kitchen in the sky, enhanced with a generous splash of wisdom, as for dessert: a plate filled with heavenly forgiveness.

Once the feasting had finished, the waiter came to present the bill and the young man paid. However, on this particular occasion the waiter stood astonished and intrigued by what he had witnessed and, on his face, twitched a gentle smile acknowledging a miracle.

The parable to this story: the restaurant establishment is the mundane existence and the young man was an innocent individual who had taken his two imaginary companions for dinner. All were seated at the same table where it was often possible to define the human character's persona in what they preferred to eat, how they socialized and communicated, and was a sign to how they thought and how they lived.

The 'ego' saw himself the king and ruler of the mind; a revengeful identity more often frustrated with anger seeking dramas to show his intent of righteousness and strength. On the other hand, the
'religious' identity was seeking redemption to in order to salvage his soul and find a place in heaven to be with God.

The higher-self, however, is the primal you, the chief, godly ambassador and it is their duty to evolve the human nature in accordance to the unchangeable, universal laws and the obedience that quickens the momentum to reach our destiny.

**

The 'restaurant waiter' is the servant who at the end of the day, presents the metaphoric bill to each patron, with the payment based on how much love/higher energy is in a person's heart; how much has been given, how much has been taken, and how much has been learned in the process.

After all, potentially, the currency in the afterlife might be based on the quality of love with human feelings being so powerful to create our reality here or elsewhere. It may be so, in the realms of reality, that each individual is seen to judge themselves on merits or failures taking ownership over their minds and how it felt to love and/or harm.

When every individual holds a personal responsibility and a duty of care toward human life, the environment, the animal kingdom, as well as unto himself, they are acknowledging that the human image is spiritual and divinely encoded with a conscience.

Therefore, it comes as no surprise, when it is up to the individual person to produce goodness, one must detach oneself from the destructive living that not only harms the soul, but pushes the world into negative territory by allowing the lower-self to remain seated at the head of the table, digesting the regular meals and repeating the same ceremonial routines. All this does is just take the Self back to the same restaurant, to the same table, to relive the same old habits. This is until the lower-self surrenders to the higher-self, to formulate a correction to free themselves from an illusionary entrapment.

CHAPTER FIVE
A MIDNIGHT DREAM

"In the midst of a silent night, the mind witnessed an incoming dream. It shared with me a magical moment; a surprising event that registered through internal vision which demonstrated the reaches of the eternal spirit."

It was time to adjust to a new reality from the way it was, to understand the way forward, and to think deeper into a conscious mind. The three-dimensional universe mainly contains a speck of realism compared to the extensions of reality, which can be accessed by an extraordinary mind to envision further chapters of eternity.

Regardless of the physical living arrangements, overdressing ourselves with the habits of yesterday, continuing to wear old, worn-out shoes, and reliving the impregnation of the past, it is in our nature to envision a reality that radiates well beyond the forces of a practical existence. Aloft in the heavens are higher dimensions that are timeless, that are futuristic in nature, as well as having a genuine affiliation with humanity's soul.

On earth, one's universe is governed by the laws of love and respect, and the spiritual cosmic laws are governed by karma's cause and effect, and through all this, the intellect's curiosity searches for the knowledge to reach its destiny. In the event to rise higher in consciousness, we need to recognize and appreciate the soul's supernatural resources to visibly detect the dimensional extensions, discovered through the ingenuity of dreams, psychic visions, and outer body experiences. We become acquainted with events that possess a certain sense of value, triggering a conscious expansion that goes well beyond the understandings of a normal rational thinking mind.

**

Supposedly, in my view, many of us have denied ourselves the reality of who we are as an evolving spirit. Maybe for superstitious reasons, we keep a pretentious distance from the truth, afraid of our true selves. We are here to develop a positive mind and not to be ruled by negative forces that undermine the full strength and the potentiality of the human spirit. The main objective in life should be the consideration to heal and strengthen the Self, for and with eternity.

We have experienced countless incarnations in order to demonstrate improvement in the Self and to create a world that is stabilized with living a truthful, honest existence. Whereby, the intellect has the freedom to create, simultaneously, the human heart and the spirit to remain connected with God within the realms of His Kingdom.

The history of the world is a manifestation created by the human mind, however, it is the spiritual that connects the soul to the universe; to implement a divine relationship between ourselves and the higher kingdoms. This is God's way to keep a holy bridge open to the universe, to allow souls to stay in touch with each other, living and deceased through, not just prayers, but within dreams- anywhere where love attracts love.

Undoubtedly, dream moments are unpredictable; not knowing what to expect until the magic happens. Dream insights can be pleasant episodes or could at times present nightmares. Above all, dreams link the human awareness to the spirit world. Dreams can also forecast present dangers; troublesome occurrences that need supernatural intervention. I remembered having this dream that connected me to a highly confronting happening. Once, in a deep sleep my mind suddenly switched to present an intervention rescue episode.

**

It was around nineteen-eighty when this happened. In those times I didn't fully understand the dream world; I thought it was just an imaginary slideshow to entertain the mind while the physical body was in stasis. But to my surprise, a day or so later I learned the accuracy of my involvement inside this supernatural episode. Here is a true account of what happened:

I saw myself on board a domestic passenger flight that was already airborne. To the rear of the plane, I saw myself slowly walking towards the captain's cabin. I was in shock and emotionally agitated, voicing my concern to the seated passengers about their impending deaths. I watched their expressions for any indication that they sensed any imminent danger but as I tried to alert them, it seemed that I was invisible to the other passengers. Still, I was deeply concerned for the safety and survival of all on board, as I knew that the plane was only a short distant away from crashing into a skyscraper.

With a sense of urgency, I walked toward the pilot's cabin trying somehow to warn him of the pending impact. I moved through the hanging curtain that divided the cockpit and the passenger section. I saw myself standing next to the pilot calling out to him in a loud voice: "You are going to crash the plane; the plane is flying too low!" Then somehow the pilot felt that something wasn't right, and I saw the plane flying straight upwards to a higher altitude just in time, avoiding a disastrous plane crash.

The plane landed safely and as I stood on the concrete tarmac a few meters away from the parked aircraft, I watched the passengers disembark down the stairway and walk towards the terminal. They walked straight passed me, their facial expressions showing a sense of fright, but also of relief to have landed safely. Then, the dream ended.

**

The next day, in the newspaper's late edition, I was surprised to see an illustrated depiction of the exact event that I had experienced in my dream the night before. The front page outlined a sketch indicating the aircraft's flight direction and showing that the plane was about five to nine kilometers away from crashing into the Empire State Building in New York City.

It was reported that the plane was flying at a very low altitude over the city in heavy, thick fog, creating poor visibility. What also didn't help was that the altitude gauge on the instrument panel was faulty. Nevertheless, the plane landed safely and in practical terms, the newspaper verified that this dream held real substance.

Around this time in early eighties, I started to have a profound interest in spiritual healing and channeling healing in conjunction with higher intelligence sources. Harry Edwards and Bruno Groening were two of the most respected and admired healers of their time and both provided miracle healings to thousands of people worldwide. I had read some of Harry Edwards books based on spiritual healing, sharing his knowledge and experiences. Harry Edwards passed away in nineteen seventy-six.

In the early nineties I had a dream encounter with Harry Edwards. There, I realized, that spiritual or divine healing can take place in the physical world as well in the spirit world while the spirit soul was still attached to the physical body. It was about five AM when the internal viewing screen was switched on, and there I found myself in search of Harry Edwards. At first, inside the astral realm of the inner space was darkness, but I felt people around me, and so I asked them where I could find the famous healer. I asked a multitude of souls but unfortunately none of them ever heard of him.

**

I became worried, as I knew that I was running out of time to continue the search. Then I happened to speak to a person that knew of Harry and told me where to find him. Within seconds I came across a small dwelling, but immediately noticed there were so many people already in line waiting to be seen. It was impossible for me to stand and wait at the end of the line so I walked forward and mentioned to the people closest to the house that my search had taken me all night and that it was only a matter of time before I would be drawn back into the awakening physical body. They agreed to allow me to be next in line to see him.

I walked into the well-lit room where Harry stood. He was finely dressed in suit pants and a white shirt folded at the sleeves and he was standing near a healing table. Then, with a stern abrupt voice, he asked me: "What do you want of me?" "A healing," I replied. I was directed onto the healing table and as he stationed himself, he tightly squeezed my ankles with his strong hands. Immediately, I felt this enormous pain gushing through my legs but strangely felt no pain in the physical body.

Right above where he stood was a bright, golden light. It pierced through the house ceiling and an intense yellowish shaft of light streamed down into the healer who began to channel the healing current through his hands. I looked down at my body and started to see all my blood vessels, arteries, and veins; the red blood being rushed at an unimaginative speed to loosen the sticky, clogged cholesterol that effectively had caused my body's high blood pressure. Then without warning, my mind's viewing screen went blank.

At that moment I was back with normal awareness and awake to a bright, sunrise light that beamed through the bedroom window. To my amazement that morning I felt re-energized with my blood pressure registering a normal reading.

**

Still to this day, I am mesmerized to have experienced a healing in the astral world with Harry Edwards. Whenever I see myself in a dream episode, the astral or light body resembles a true replica of my physical body features. In turn, both the spirit body and the physical body are capable of receiving divine healings on different states of reality when a healing is required.

Bruno Groening is another extraordinary and influential healer with whom I respect and greatly admire. He was often referred to as the miracle healer. Bruno travelled throughout Germany and Austria creating the *Bruno Groening Circle of Friends* that has grown into one of the largest spiritual organizations worldwide.

The spiritual gatherings, promoted healing and meditation sessions, reminding people to stay on the spiritual path. Bruno taught that God was behind all healings and that he was an instrument; a bridge to channel the divine healing stream to the sick. Sadly, Bruno passed away in nineteen fifty-nine at the age of fifty-three.

Two extraordinary healers, Harry Edwards and Bruno Groening- one lived in England the other in Germany, both gave thousands of sufferers a return to health and wholeness. They both demonstrated the existence of a higher power, a Divine Source that heals.

What also should be respected and acknowledged is the vital influence shared through our health system; the doctors surgeons, nurses, and health specialists, all with their individual skills who are committed to saving lives, treating illnesses, mending broken bones, carrying out surgery- all wonderful souls who are healing the physical and mental afflictions that can impact a person's life.

CHAPTER SIX
DEATH HAS NO DEATH

"The body had taken the final breath, the physical landscape had disappeared from sight, the transition phase from one reality to another had been unavoidable… As a beam of light uplifted the spirit from the physical domain to be taken back home to live amongst the billions of stars that nightly twinkled in the above heavens, sharing special moments with us to forget me not."

The complexity associated with death and dealing with bereavement is something that is very rarely spoken about. No doubt a sensitive and emotional subject to envision, especially in not knowing what to expect for both the grievers and the departed soul.

The heart becomes inflamed with the grief of missing a loved departed soul. The human light that has left the family and close friends behind is a painful time for all involved, including the deceased. The once bright days are changed to dark clouds and are filled with the pouring rain of weeping tears, awaiting the day that the pain will heal.

The mind and heart are taunted with memories replacing the touch of a human soul. In the days following there will be a funeral whereby the body will be buried, and the preacher will tell the congregation that the person has gone to Heaven. Inside the chapel, the grief is felt as the internal words try in vain to make sense of the despair. "Unexpectedly sadness arrived at my door and told me I had lost the person I most adored. Uncontrollable feelings, fueled by this dreadful shock have unbalanced my mind. As tears rush down both cheeks, my whole body was shaking like a leaf.

**

I still can't understand why this has happened; to suffer like this, I mean why is the pain punishing me? Dear God, have I lost strength and faith in Thee? A bright light has been extinguished and left me with uncertainties. All I needed from you was to have stayed with me, to share the life we once knew. But now I can't even imagine that you are not here anymore… still awaiting an empty room and for you walk through the front door."

Lonely hours spent clinging to a ticking clock, then, one evening while reminiscing and recalling the way it once was, I felt a cold shiver. It was if someone was with me and I heard these words within my mind that sounded so familiar to me: "Don't be afraid, everything will be alright. Never think that you have lost me, you know that love can never be separated from love, and nothing has the power to stop us or pull us apart. There is really nothing to worry about, nothing has changed between us, just my physical body came to an end and now I am free and can choose to look after you."

Then, the room went silent, and I found myself at peace. The pain and hurt had lifted as I wiped the tears away. The grief had brought me closer to my soul and I started to feel human and special again, thinking of, and being grateful for, the moments we had together. As expected, the physical body can't live on forever; there comes the unwanted day to say our goodbyes as the earthbound mission comes to an end and it's time for Scotty to 'beam us up' and take us home to where we belong.

The body has a death, but the spirit has no death. Death and separation are an illusion as there is no *death* in death. The departed souls on the other side of life, continue to live with feelings, desires, habits, beliefs, self-interests in the way woman or man are manifested on earth.

**

There is nothing that can be done to change the way it just is, the situation with life, death, and the transition phases. Whoever we are born to, in a certain country, whoever we choose to create a family with, what is endeared and treasured, will eventually lead us back to what we thought was lost; memories carried inside the human heart.

After my mother passed away, and in the chapel during her funeral service in the vacant seat in the front row, I noticed a spirit apparition in her image, dressed in her favorite attire and sitting silently. She was watching her own funeral.

The following night in my dream I saw both of us together walking down a long corridor as I guided her toward a particular door. The door opened and inside the room she was greeted with familiar faces; family, relatives, uncles, aunts, everyone that you could imagine was there to celebrate her home coming. I entered the room with her when suddenly the dream ended.

On another funeral occasion, I saw the deceased woman's spirit walking invisibly amongst the congregation, shaking hands, and saying her last goodbyes to her friends. Often with spiritual sight, the spirit can be seen witnessing their own funeral, in acknowledgement that they had died, to share final moments with their loved ones, and to be shown how much they are respected.

Early one day I encountered an unusual, unexpected visitor. The time was precisely six in the morning when I was awakened by the sound of a pre-set alarm clock.

**

Since I still had few moments left before I needed to dress and go to work, my mind remained half asleep. Although my daydreaming eyes remained closed, my awareness was alert when a vision appeared, and I saw a slender woman clothed in a grey tracksuit, standing in the midst of what looked like a night's sky. I heard her voice asking me if I wanted to go for a jog and in my mind, I said: "Yes" thinking that I could use the exercise.

Immediately when I had this thought, I saw both of us travelling into what seemed to be the cosmos. As the journey continued, I felt frustrated knowing that I could travel at a much faster speed than this seemingly slow jog and it was then that I realized that I was a distance ahead of her. I heard her calling out not to go that quick, and at that moment she was back by my side.

Suddenly, I felt immense exhaustion as thought I couldn't manage to go any further. Now travelling at a walking pace, we finally reached a borderline from the darkness. Then, we stepped out onto a magnificent, bright, green countryside that had appeared before us. Looking downwards from the high hills, my sight was automatically focused on a distant red brick building as I spotted a woman carrying blankets into what seemed to be a boarding house.

Then, I noticed that I was standing alone as my travelling companion who guided me here had mysteriously departed. Also, intuitively at that moment, I sensed that my father was living inside this building. Within seconds I saw myself inside the house, and I found myself resting against the walls where several bunk beds were positioned. In the middle of the room there was a square table and I saw my father seated playing cards with other individuals. My father had died many years before my mother had passed away.

**

I stood there in silence for a few moments observing the sight before my father noticed me. He sprung up from his seat and was surprised that I was in the same room with him. We both greeted each other with great joy, smiles, and tears and we hugged, appreciating this momentous reunion. Then my mind told me that I needed to get dressed to be on time for work.

In time, I tried to assess the meaning or reason I was taken to see my father, where he was and in that moment of his life. The only conclusion that came to mind was an illustration that family members remain connected with each other no matter the separations of time or distance… that love rules.

In the same pattern concerning domestic pets, all animals who have passed away also come under the one umbrella of love. They express their own personality, intelligence and have feelings towards their owners. Pets and animals also have an afterlife and a special place in the spirit world where they await to be reunited with the one(s) that loved them.

I remember both the day I lost my beloved dog and the day a close friend of mine had to put down her golden Labrador who had suffered from cancer. I was there when the vet gave the injection; it was a sorrowful moment to witness as she said goodbye to her long-time companion who had a beautiful gentle friendly personality. You could tell that the pet also knew what was happening to him. He laid there unmoved with sadness as he gently closed his eyes and passed away peacefully.

That night I felt the loss and the sadness that had overshadowed a difficult day, when finally, I fell asleep. During that time, I had a remarkable dream where I saw myself in the astral realm, unaware of where I was. Suddenly, I stood in front of a beautiful peaceful, magical place where the landscape was covered with green manicured lawns. There I saw the resting place for deceased pet dogs, divided in countless rows where each pet had their own small space to be rested.

**

The atmosphere bloomed with serenity and quietness. As I stepped forward to enter this gigantic encampment, two angelic guardians who stood guard, protecting this heavenly place, approached me and softly mentioned that I shouldn't be there. I quickly explained that I was there to see the golden Labrador named "Bruiser who had just passed away, and my beloved kelpie Sindy." I asked if they were there. They nodded and led me where Bruiser was resting and I noticed that his owner was already there, cuddling his golden body, his tail briskly wagging with joy.

The guardians who protected this particular animal region said that the new arrivals are placed near the gateway entrance, that the rows are determined by how long they had been there. They told me that each pet would rest peacefully, waiting for day to be reunited with their owners in the spirit world and that the unclaimed ones at some stage will be reborn to find a permanent meaningful attachment with a new owner.

I asked the guardian if I could see my dog Sindy whom I had lost when I was a young adult living in a country town. The guardian without hesitation guided me much further down the line. I saw her immediately. She also noticed me and jumped up with excitement running towards me. It was magical moment of joy embracing the black body fringed with a white patch under her neck. Rekindling a friendship that had been sorely missed for many years. All night, I dreamt being with my friend on that level of reality, and even the next day my mind was still visualizing the priceless reunion.

What this connection demonstrated, was that what is loved, treasured, and remains attached to our heart, be it people or pets, will always be found again.

CHAPTER SEVEN
SEDUCED BY A MUNDANE ILLUSION

*"Human civilization's ingenuity is kept inside
an enormous deception trap that tricks the human intellect
to remain psychologically detained by a materialistic
simulation that tends to imprison its own Self."*

On frequent occasions, mainly Sunday mornings, I would visit the city harbor to spend time with my thoughts. In relaxation mode I would take in and admire the enclosed natural serenity. The nearly encircled waters harbored luxurious anchored sailing yachts, birthed fishing trawlers and smaller charter boats that gave the view a pleasant, relevant character.

Beneath a blue sky, I would see people walking along concreted walkways with a sense of normality, enjoying the freedom to spend precious moments engaging in friendly chatter with family and close friends and enjoying each other's company.

Here, I thought, as much as the natural world is beautiful, contrastingly one's experience of it is largely tormented by the oppression of greed and debts that have created a wider divide between the common people and the profiteers. Ultimately, in many cases vulnerable families are pushed into poverty and homelessness.

How could anyone have imagined greed becoming more important than life itself? Inducing a civilization to become seduced by a monopolized deception, envisioned to enslave the common people. What was meant to be a fair, honorable, dignified, humane, developing world has instead been transformed into a problematic curse, where most people have found themselves constantly plagued with so many insecure uncertainties, leaving families unable to cope- trying to exist without a proper, regular financial income.

**

How can human intelligence create an unstable environment? How can sanity breed insanity? How is it that so many people are now suffering with mental illness? What profits a man when the world around him is falling apart? How much longer can the human heart endure the pain, discomfort and struggles created by a disfigured, disorientated establishment?

As I sat there, I would also ponder, love, compassion, and the selflessness of people to support each other, especially in times of need. Life has a conscience, a meaning, a purpose, and endurance. What is wrong with creating a world where there is no hunger, no poverty, no condemnation and where all people are living in equality? It would mean a positive turnaround to make this planet a stable and enjoyable livable experience instead of humanity remaining frustrated and filled with fears and anger. How can people trust the world to be safe, secure and to provide a brighter future for them?

There is only one human race; one choice and one opportunity to live in togetherness as human beings, for us all to have a decent, respectable, creative, and prosperous humane experience. The human mind is so powerful it can improve living conditions, or it can destroy people's lives, and this is the reality that so many people and families are living. People are hurting and suffering in silence, hanging onto prayers of hope for deliverance and waiting for the chance to be freed from the valley of death.

From the beginning, the way of life was meant to be a spiritual journey. Our lives were meant to be an evolutionary process to gain more consciousness in order to express the higher nature of the spirit. Instead, people have mostly inherited thunderstorms, confronting, bitter, cold winds, and a reality smitten with deceptions, dishonesty, illusions, and fantasies that act to seduce and divert the human intellect from living an honorable, dignified, progressive existence.

**

Overall, there is a pretentious reality for the profiteers and the real world of the people, that humankind only wants to be treated fairly and justly to make an honest living. To have a comfortable timeframe to unfold the human nature to achieve the highest effect of discovering the real you. We need to share influential intelligence and we need to connect with other people; living is created by the people for the people.

But the illusion of reality that now stands at people's doors is a world in distress; a world that is in need of help. A world that seemed mostly to have lost its soul and direction in life.

To have a physical working experience, to express individual skillful preferences, to develop the spiritual mind to free the Self from the reincarnation cycle… this is the main purpose to achieve and to unchain the human mind from an artificial, invented illusion. Spirituality is the magical force that enables the Self to see past a mundane exercise in the true sense, to rediscover his divinity his natural state of immortality.

What then makes a spiritual person? What does it mean for me to live with a conscience, to live an honest peaceful respectable life? How do we define a person who is always in search for the truth, who cares for the wellness of humanity, for the planet, and a person that sees no sense to harm or to destroy life?

This is a person who can be trusted, who has a strong belief in God, who always remembers that he belongs to an afterlife.

I like to tell a story that is symbolic in nature and a reflection that would give the Self the opportunity to save himself from the illusion. At the center of this imaginary insight stands a gigantic monument that resembles a mysterious money tree that has become the cornerstone that controls the human civilization.

**

This tree produced an automatically continuous amount of green paper money, that attracted people's mind to be drawn to this tree as if a vast spell had been cast to bewitch the captives to fall into a hypnotic entrancement system. The tree's protruding roots fastened themselves firmly into the earth's soil so it would manifest a richer life for some or a poorer life for others. The swampy land that surrounded the money tree was almost an illusion; where people were made only to see what was to become a spiritual diversion to fasten themselves to an imprisonment of materialistic stimulation.

The entire world had now relied on this tree for their survival. I saw people in a rush to climb the outstretched branches to grab whatever they could to feel safe or to feed an inborn desire of materialistic success. In fact, the tree held so much influence creating an altered ego in a person, that one stood apart from his higher persona. In such case, the Self, became his own victim where he could only envision his success and happiness based on the accumulation of wealth, to live for a few fleeting moments in a state of prominence.

As I thought this, I suddenly saw myself amongst the crowd rushing towards this magical tree, feeling the same needs, desires, and excitement. During the rush, I thought that this could be an instigated financial trap where the individual has no other means to survive but to allow himself to become a prisoner, chained and shackled to the money tree; forsaking his freedom just to make a sensible living.

By now I was in readiness to climb the lower branches when suddenly I stumbled and fell over a protruding tree root. I landed on the sticky mud, and I lay there for a few moments looking stunned and embarrassed. Then, from nowhere, a hand reached down to me, assisting me to stand upright again. The stranger pointed to a narrow pathway, implying to follow.

**

The path led to a nearby lagoon and for a brief moment I stood by the water's edge sighting an anchored, sailing yacht that awaited me to board. I turned around wanting to thank the stranger, but I noticed that I was now all alone to continue my journey. I boarded the yacht and unfastened the vessel from its mooring in readiness to sail. Two white sails captured a fair breeze that propelled the boat's keel to slice its way through the waterline and head toward an open sea.

Then a strange thing happened. Immediately, the whole scenery changed; a modern city harbor appeared, and the shoreline was flanked with high-rise apartments, corporate offices, and international motels. In the midst of their shadows, languished businesses, shops, café, and other eateries, while on the water's edge, the ferry system commuted the daily workers and tourists to their desired destinations.

The yacht was picking up speed, sailing through the harbor making a fine run towards the open heads that partially separated the inner waters from its main source- the open sea. The vessel reached the heads, and the tall masts were overshadowed on both sides by the imposing sandstone cliffs as the yacht's bow passed through the narrow passageway to sail into the beyond.

I briefly gazed back towards a disappearing mainland as the yacht left a waving, whitish trail in its wake. The mighty cliffs proudly guarded the harbor entrance and vanished into the far distance. On one side of the clifftop stood the political and financial fortress, while on the other side, cemented into the rock, stood the mighty, majestical religions–between them gave the nation a sense of trust, security, and authenticity.

Sailing on the high seas with a new sunrise in the far, eastern sky I sensed the natural warmth and forgotten sense of freedom to treasure being in oneness with the universe.

**

On board I felt a calmness and the ocean and I both shared the one freedom; a difference in being tied to mainland, unrest living. The sailing vessel continued to slice its way through the peaceful waterline as I focused my attention on meditating and seeking inspirations in order to reach my destiny.

Then I heard a gentle, soft inner voice that spoke to me in an idealistic way: "All is what it is, you have got to stand up for things that are sensible, for all that heals the world and that which connects with the truth. People are the farmers, the planters planting their crops inside the fields of the mind. Knowledge is the fertilizer that enriches growth; whatever is planted in the Self is reaped and that then becomes a self-image – a reflection of you. Collectively, one would need both the sunshine and the rains to allow the growing seeds to reach full maturity.

What is sown becomes the harvest- the food that feeds the soul; it either enriches the spirit soul with unconditional love, kindness, goodwill, or with negative food in being recklessness. The conscious planter has the choice to plant a healthy harvest or in ignorance plant a mixture of weeds."

Late evening was fast approaching, and the signs were visible in the sky as I looked beyond the bow where I could see, in the near distance, an outstretched landscape that seemed to invite the yacht to make landfall. I sailed into a seashore bay to anchor the boat. What was important to me was that I had found my inner peace, but I also knew that the mundane reality was a stepping foundation to bring forth the best or the worst in what humanity can produce.

CHAPTER EIGHT
CAUGHT THE WRONG TRAIN TO NOWHERE

"Has a civilized world come to an end or is there still some magic left in its soul? Somehow the intellectuals have guided the human population into another reality of total dependency dominated by the computerized electronic age."

Living has become very different now, permanently changed from the old fashion days where people lived in a natural way, where they interacted, communicated, and responded to the old ways of life. There was no internet, no digital devices, and no household computers… people lived a simple, orderly life.

Now it is a very different world where people's minds are reprogrammed to function in accordance with the age of technology. Where comprehensively, human interactions in the business world, rely upon the functions of a keyboard and various electronic devices connected to the internet, where people's fingers do the talking and communicating.

We are at a crucial moment where a stronger belief has arisen; yet we continue to live in a consumerist reality that has no divine sanction; where our minds and lives endeavor to advance in a materialistic civilization. We are born to be different naturally, yet we continue to fail in our attempts to live in a humane way, to feel 'human' and thus enjoy the genuine, incentive continuation of soul fulfilment, that emerges with the essential substance of who we truly are.

**

But perhaps there is a good reason for the way it is, after all technology has its merits. However, the problem arises when we abandon the art of natural communication between society, family, and friends. We divide ourselves further apart from our potential- our spiritual consciousness. No matter on what platform we stand on, we are constantly engaged in an unfinished, psychological, and spiritual duet, that unfolds our divine nature… our real reason for living.

What is for certain is that we can't resign from life, no matter what the universe has given us to deal with. We can't escape the consequences of our actions. What has been created becomes a reality, a fact of life. What we never should forsake is the capability to love, to acknowledge that the human persona is supernatural in nature, and that we each inhibit unimaginable psychic, healing powers.

Normalization and equality should remain the footprint of humanity. No doubt the light will always shine, and the darkness will have its moment to confuse and brush aside its negativity. Nevertheless, we all should appreciate the time we have; to be grateful for the opportunity to live, to raise a family and to dream of the future.

Humanity has inherited a world in progress, a new age where electronic technology and computerization has made a large difference. On so many levels, this advancement has been a great benefit to mankind. On the negative front, technology is being used to promote the manufacturing of nuclear weapons that have the potential to destroy the world.

**

We are living in a time where we must come to realize that we are designed to be the creators of love and peace, not the creators of doom and destruction. With this thought in my mind, a psychic image appeared that told a story outlying the sequences of two choices.

In this scene there were two passenger trains that stood stationary at central station. On Platform Nine and Ten, people awaited in readiness to board the carriages. Here, they had only a brief moment to decide which train they wished to board.

The train on Platform Nine, now fully loaded with passengers, started to pull away from the station platform as an announcement was broadcast over the interior speakers: "Welcome on board. This is the train of progress. Destination, 'Brick Wall Station'."

In the leading carriages, upon settling in their seats, passengers began to open their laptops while others were occupied with their smart phones. As the train travelled away from the city, people's minds were tightly glued to their devices, unaware of the scenery that flashed passed them outside of the train's window.

Moments later, the train's conductor walked throughout each carriage and stamped each passenger with a microchip, assisted by a medical practitioner whose job it was to inject all passengers with a newly developed COVID-19 vaccine – a compulsory requirement to remain on the train.

**

Passengers were also required to pay the train fare by credit card as cash was no longer accepted.

In the middle carriages, these passengers were bemused with digital gaming devices, with some games so destructive in nature, that the players were completely unaware of the demoralizing effect they were having on human nature.

In the following carriages, were the movie directors, producers, and actors who gave the world an imaginary illusion, the impersonation of heroes and scoundrels. A pretense written script that mostly exhibited fictional behaviorism.

By now, the train had travelled quite a long distance when it made a quick stop to allow the robotic generation to board. The walking, talking, sophisticated, and programmable humanoid robots were designed to imitate humans and were operated to respond by verbal commands.

The humanoid robots waltzed down through the carriage corridor to be seated. The unimaginable had been created and yet had been welcomed into the human household. There was no longer the need to cook good, wholesome meals, clean the house, wash clothes, take the children to school… the robot generation had been designed and destined to take over the world.

The end carriage contained the bleakest time in human history. Seated in this this carriage were the ungodly minds; the engineering technicians who designed and gave countries nuclear weapons, under the pretense for people to feel safer.

**

Eventually a final broadcast came through the carriage speakers announcing that the train will shortly terminate at the next stop,

Brick Wall Station. The train began to slow and then stopped, signaling the end of the journey. As the doors opened, each passenger vacated the train and they stepped into a reality where all electronic devices and credit cards were confiscated by cemetery gate keepers. No material items were to proceed beyond the graveyard.

Meanwhile, the train on Platform Ten had by now pulled away from the station with passengers who wanted to live with a conscience in a humane way, and to remain as natural as possible. These were people who loved nature, loved family life, and loved the world.

Not long after the train left the station, an announcement was broadcast, welcoming everyone aboard the journey towards 'Paradise Junction'. The train travelled at speed through the city suburbs, and passengers acquainted themselves in friendship with each other. They all seemed to be similar in nature; good-hearted people that believed in conscious living, growing, and expanding the infinite mind as a manifestation of divinity.

They believed in the powers of the spirit; that all people are intuitively minded healers and psychics. They believed in themselves, and they believed in peace and human rights. But most interestingly, they all had a good sense of humor, optimism, and hope. The length of the train radiated with a bright, golden aura; a shimmering light that reflected a genuine level of soul advancement.

**

The passengers were open-minded, respectable souls; friendly light workers that symbolized the importance of compassion. They embodied a combination of love and hope.

One final instruction was heard through the carriage speakers, announcing that the train will terminate at the next stop: Paradise Junction. It said that for the passengers who wished to continue beyond this station, they would need to board an adjoining train to travel further into the realms of spiritual consciousness.

CHAPTER NINE
HUMANITY AND HEAVEN

"The human individual stood intrigued with the quest, in search of life's higher meaning. Desire for the mind to find the truth and for the heart to connect with the forces of love, as the human spirit evolves to rescue itself from an illusionary deception."

Here we are stuck on a planet isolated from the kingdom of Heaven, living in a world seeded with fears, ignorance, judgements, and self-induced hysteria that intend to keep a soul trapped in the lower levels of consciousness while awaiting the miracle that can elevate us to an invisible paradise.

What we have is a practical, spiritual solution that is designed for the Self to come to terms with their own reality to realize what is being created from their own mind. When in fact, the core of reality is a progressive, continuous, informative, experience that one experiences until the last doorway to eternal freedom is reached.

Our world is in pain, suffering from the lack of spiritual light. The darkness is filled with deception, fallacies, and greed leaving vulnerable souls exposed to human injustice. Nonetheless, we exist in a time of correction; a wake-up, self-realization moment wherein exists the opportunity to enrich the Self with a higher form of intelligence and being.

**

For the world to enliven its soul, we must evolve beyond the fortress of pain and suffering into a reality that is mindful and wiser to understand the reality of the Self. It makes me wonder if the mainstream population has been fooled into being fearful and disorientated in order to distance ourselves from our divine nature.

Now we see a world in a mess; a battle between solidarity and divisions, peace and war, hunger and greed. All this may be due to an 'unawareness state'; an imbalance between the human mind and soul-wise consciousness. Instead of striving to be who we are meant to be, we live a life afraid to travel on the road that leads to recovery and wholeness.

In my mind, there is nothing wrong with a person striving for the truth; one seeking to enrich the mind with self-enlightenment. We have an opportunity to experience the ascension of our consciousness and to educate ourselves about the higher frequency of love and life. We have the opportunity to stand higher in the cosmic universe, to create in our own world, internally and outwardly, a place where peace and humility can survive.

If we don't we will stay adrift as prisoners, encircled by temptations, personal conflicts and all the other nonsense which is destined to turn an earthly life into a dreadful nightmare.

**

On an individual level, we have the liberty to express our own free-will, taking charge of our destiny. In the spiritual sense, we can remain in control of the pathway that can provide us with the best advancement into the fields of eternity.

In my experience, life hasn't always been easy. For many of us, the cards of life that we have been dealt were intended to bring forth emotional triggers to inspire personal growth. Lessons, that at times are very uncomfortable to bear, challenging the Self to look beyond the tears and feelings of hopelessness and desperation.

We each have our own road to conquer. These roads are precariously blocked with unforeseen problematic obstacles: stop signs, hazards, twists, and turns that could drive a person mentally and emotionally insane.

There was a time when walking, I drove straight into a roadblock leading to a painful readjustment in my life. It took place on a particular afternoon when I was feeling emotionally distraught and just wanted to release all the hurt inside of me.

I soon came to realize that the pain caused by the roadblock was not an accident. It stood as a reminder that I have the ability to choose which path I can take. A moment later, a vision came to me. The episode contained a combination of talking pictures that left a lasting impression on my mind; insights that gave me back balance, strength, and hope, in knowing that the universe hadn't forgotten me.

**

The supernatural sequences began when I heard an inner voice that spoke of peace and goodwill; I was told whoever drinks from my cup shall have the blessings of everlasting life. It said: "On the mountain high, stood a kingdom with cities of light that gloried the countryside. At the center of the city, stood a golden temple to which the Holy Chalice rested on its alter. This contained the sacred waters of everlasting life."

Upon hearing these words, intuitively, I knew that the Lord, Jesus Christ was speaking. Then the spoken words continued: "It was noticed from above, that the valley below, was without love and stands in darkness. It was filled with sorrow and pain, so much so that God could no longer bear to witness this, so God spoke, and all the Angels in Heaven stood still. The time had come to sacrifice His Son."

"Go down into the valley to save my people, for they have forgotten how to love, they have forgotten to live peacefully, and how to believe in living a spiritual life that would have set them free. My people have forgotten to believe in Me." Upon his descent into the Valley of Man, he said: "People please listen to me for I speak with authority" and as the people began to flock at his feet, he said: "Let us now begin the difficult climb."

The following vision reflected the rescue and I witnessed multitude of people following the Lord from the valley along an uphill track.

**

After travelling a short distance, they reached a narrow wooden bridge. Just before the pathways of the bridge met, I heard the Lord's voice pleading not tread on them, yet with sadness, some did not listen, and they were led back down the two separate pathways to the tears and unrest of the lower valley. The others who followed the Lord crossed the wooden bridge. The climb was hard, and the people became thirsty and very tired. The Lord told the followers to rest for a while and to face the mountain side.

The followers knelt and instantly were blessed, and as numerous water springs began to flow, they drank and were satisfied. I then saw them continue the climb, and before them, they saw the mountain's summit where the City of Lights stood. Then, suddenly, the supernatural vision ended. With interest and curiosity, I wanted to further explore the meaning of this vision. Despite this, I have interpreted this vision as below:

The valley was the human world, controlled by the lower-self where souls were trapped and consumed by various beliefs, systems, traditional customs, and day-to-day routine. It was a place where the greatest sins are conceived to live a dishonest life and to betray and torture each other. Here is where people had separated themselves from the truth, and a human bond with God was broken. A savior was sent from Heaven to give salvation to the lost and deliverance back to God. The mountain climb reflected the journey through the various levels of consciousness, an ascension path to the Golden Temple where the higher-self claimed residency.

**

Just before the narrow bridge, on either side, two sign posts stood. One was signposted: "*Passion*" and the other: "*Desire*". People were warned not to tread on these paths for they would only lead you back down into the valley of birth and death.

The bridge they crossed was built on the pillars of faith, and on the climb, they rested and drank from the waters of knowledge that nourished the mind and soul. The city above was the Father's Kingdom that beamed with endless love and that enriched souls with eternal life.

In conclusion, the human experience is an attempt to produce consciousness. An opportunity to learn the required lessons to give the mind a taste of living conditions, experiencing fleeting epiphany moments to allow for revelations to inspire the Self toward self-enlightenment.

Each of us have a journey that can widen the scope of awareness between the Self and the Universe and the You with God. In developing the powers of the spirit, the highest accomplishment one can achieve is one that enables the spirit and soul to astral travel beyond the physical boundary to be united with another world.

CHAPTER TEN
THE FINAL DISCLOSURE

*"Spirituality is a special honor,
a divine gift that only you can give to yourself in order to
realize the greater part of Self and to walk the enlightened path
towards the highest possible point of eternity."*

Over many years I had captured life's enduring trials and tribulations, of joy and heart aches, but in reality, my journey had given my mind a greater awareness, stability, openness, dreamscapes, and supernatural visions.

Each of these experiences have produced memories that have shaped my human, spiritual character. Though as my expected physical life nears its end, I know that my soul has progressed beyond what I am able to dictate. What I do know, however, is throughout the measure of time, I have had the opportunity to evaluate the challenges of life, and gain an understanding of my internal world, my own mind, and my own heart. I have grown to know and understand my Self and why we are here.

I have learned more about myself and my inner universe not in spite of, but, in part, due to the ordeals that have shaped my character in my discovery. However, make no mistake, living in an imperfect world isn't easy, when the Self must exist in accordance with whatever is placed before us. What I have learned, is the best way to survive is by knowing your state of spirituality.

**

It is the 'you' who defines the human character. It is not the mind, tarnished with mainstream propaganda and programming. It is the 'you' which collectively upholds the wellbeing of the soul. Spirituality always helps to foster a positive character to succeed in the search for wisdom and to live a life full of love, trust, and honesty.

The enlightenment path, that unites us in togetherness, creates solidarity amongst us all. We live in a progressive timeline that allows us to, collectively and individually, open our minds to receiving new inspirations and enable the imagination to take you from here to eternity.

This became clear to me on my self-discovery journey where I had learned about the ways of the spirit, gained more insight to the afterlife, recognized that we all possess spiritual and psychic powers, gained an internal viewing channel via the third eye- all which helped to strengthen formal communication with the Divine.

This enables the Self to gain personal knowledge in having a flirtation with destiny; evaluating the lost pages of life, where the findings improve what the mind can actually comprehend in terms of a consideration of merit, commonsense and eternalness.

From a spiritual and human perspective, what matters in the timeframe given to every individual, is to become aware of the power we each possess to emerge beyond the broader picture of life and living.

**

What is important to recognize is that we are preparing ourselves for the afterlife, so we can achieve the highest possible outcome in the Kingdom of Heaven. To think that happiness depends on the accumulation of material wealth is a fallacy. We were born to live a constructive, meaningful life that has soul.

I have gained so many understandings and insights to what occurs in the next life. Whereby, upon arrival into the afterlife, the spirit of a person with a good heart, filled with humility and selflessness will find a paradise where the environmental landscape is enriched with exquisite beauty, majestical waterfalls, clear lakes, flowing rivers, village farmlands surrounded by green pastures and where the days are glowing in sunshine. It will be a peaceful place where family and friends are reunited to celebrate their graduation and accomplishments.

However, in a much lower, darker density, the energy frequency is very different. The astral terrain is covered with swampland

and the atmosphere is doomed with coldness. The realm is occupied by souls, who, whilst alive on Earth, produced wickedness, deliberately destroying human life, causing enormous pain and suffering to others. It is such in the afterlife they would inherit a reminder the consequences of their actions.

There is no escape from the laws of karma, it knows each person's reality to have lived in judgement or to have lived with love.

**

One must also be mindful that we have been entrusted to return to God. In connection with this, is a reminder that all of us are involved in the same storyline, on the same climb, to attain a natural ascendancy in consciousness.

In my life I often thought about the past, ruminating over the mistakes made plus also reminding myself of the all the good I produced. I dreamt mostly every night, inspired by supernatural visions, guided by Spirit being an intuitive spiritual healer, and this gave me a sense of inner peace and contentment to live in harmony with the Universe, with God.

Still, I possessed the interest and the maturity to venture beyond the walls of normality, knowing that I am a realist believing in the truth and all that I detect, supernaturally or otherwise, becomes my reality.

Here, I would like to share with you, a spiritual revelation that I received from spirit, an insight which foresaw the final disclosure of the finality of human fulfilment. The vision appeared on the mind's viewing screen and there I saw myself high atop a mountain, standing on a protruding ledge, looking downward over an outstretched countryside.

There, I noticed that the entire astral scenery glowed with an enriched, golden color that gave the landscape a pleasant, heavenly outlook.

**

Below, I saw a dirt road that weaved through the valley grounds, and I saw that the full length of road was covered with people all slowly walking in the same direction. At the end of the road, I noticed a brightly, vibrant, golden orb - an exact image that would characterize a celestial sun that stretched from ground level into the midway heights of the skyline.

It was a magical sight to behold, with numerous souls and a heavenly gateway that gave light to the whole countryside. As I gazed upon this sight, a person clothed in a white robe suddenly appeared next to me, he too gazing towards the valley below. I noticed that he had brown eyes and his face was covered with a whitish beard. His soul seemed to beam with a hint of love and wisdom. I soon became aware that the stranger was a Master, and I was to be his student.

From our vantage point we could easily see each soul walking in the direction towards this gigantic, golden, circular portal all wearing similar brownish, baggy robes. All the people that I saw had lengthy unkempt beards and their faces were wrinkled with old age. It was as though their journey had been long and exhausting- both mentally and physically.

At this point, the dialog with the Master commenced and I was given a lesson to comprehend what all this meant. As his student I started asking the questions.

**

"Master, who are those souls all yearning to reach the golden light at the road's end?" I asked. As the Master replied I sensed the compassion in his voice: "They all have the right to be here to complete their spiritual journey."

Then, within a split second, the Master and I were walking amongst these souls, us too dressed in brown robes like them, the only difference being that ours were neater and less worn.

The Master quickly replied: "My son, this road leads to the gates of Heaven. The souls you see before you have earned the right to progress along this road to reach their final destination." My immediate thought was that a snail could walk quicker, but then I suddenly felt ashamed to even think in this way. I replied: "Master, they all seem to be very tired, struggling even to walk. These souls look to be the poorest of the poor, and have absolutely nothing in their possession, only a wooden staff to assist them as they walk."

The soft, gentle spoken voice said: "My son, to travel along this pathway, one must first seek the freedom from temptations and not to allow endless desires to rule one's life. No material wealth can be taken with you along this path, so please do not judge them, but consider them for who they are and not by means of how much wealth has been acquired… for all these illusions do pass away."

**

The Master continued: "My son, do not see them with earthly eyes, judge them not. To you they appear to be the poorest of the poor with only their clothing accredited to them, but if you were to look again closely with your spiritual eye, you will notice quite clearly the brilliance of their souls that are full of light and hearts filled with so much love. Throughout each of their lifetimes, through trials and errors they have kept their faith in God. They have conquered the lower-self, they have served the world unconditionally, and they shared kindness, mercy and forgiveness."

Upon hearing those words, I still wasn't completely convinced that the the souls had a right to be there. The Master teacher quickly responded with empathy in his voice supporting the entitlement to enter into Heaven: "You seem to be confused about their personal achievements, my son. There, before you are thousands of souls making their way towards the entrance into Heaven. Take a good look and choose anyone of these souls you see before you and I will say to you, without any doubt, that they would give up their life for you." And with those words, the revelation ended.

Returning to normal reality, and reviewing the lesson, I realized my involvement with the Spiritual Master as his student was to raise questions, to work through what I was seeing, and to advance my knowing regarding the ultimate destiny of the spirit.

**

The experience overall, also gave my mind an awareness that we are all part of the human story. We have an opportunity to emerge on the same page with God, to become free from the physical re-incarnation cycle solving past and present karma, and to perfect human nature by developing the powers of the spirit. It requires wisdom to rescue the higher-self from the fortress of the lower mind; one that has caused so many discomforts, misfortunes, and divisions amongst the human civilization and to realize that this wisdom exists in each of us.

We are on a mission to evolve with knowledge in shaping our destiny, to find freedom and inner peace. By discovering the real You, you will find the place where God lives.

** The End **

About The Author
Bernard Thiemann

Bernard was born in Germany 1949. When he was seven years of age, he arrived in Australia with his family only to return to Germany at 14, where he obtained a qualification as a boilermaker and welder.

Upon completion of his apprenticeship, Bernard returned to Australia and worked in his field of trade for 28 years. During this time, Bernard was drawn towards cultivating his spiritual nature. In 1981, he became involved in volunteer work, training and then working as a telephone counsellor for five years.

As a result, Bernard developed a deep desire to become a spiritual, intuitive healer; attending meditation sessions and spiritualist church services where he gained vital, spirit knowledge. It was at this time that Bernard saw the importance for self-enlightenment. As a healer, Bernard provided a universal bond between himself, the patient, and Source.

Throughout his adult life, he also realized the importance of furthering a practical-spiritual application in order to enhance a rise in consciousness, one being this book. His goal: to help to expose a greater understanding of who we are and our inborn greatness that holds the power to unravel the secrets of creation.

www.ingramcontent.com/pod-product-compliance
Lightning Source LLC
Chambersburg PA
CBHW030301010526
44107CB00053B/1777

9780648697459